HOODWINKER

THE SIN OF CHEATING YOUR SELF

KAAVYAA TRIVEDI

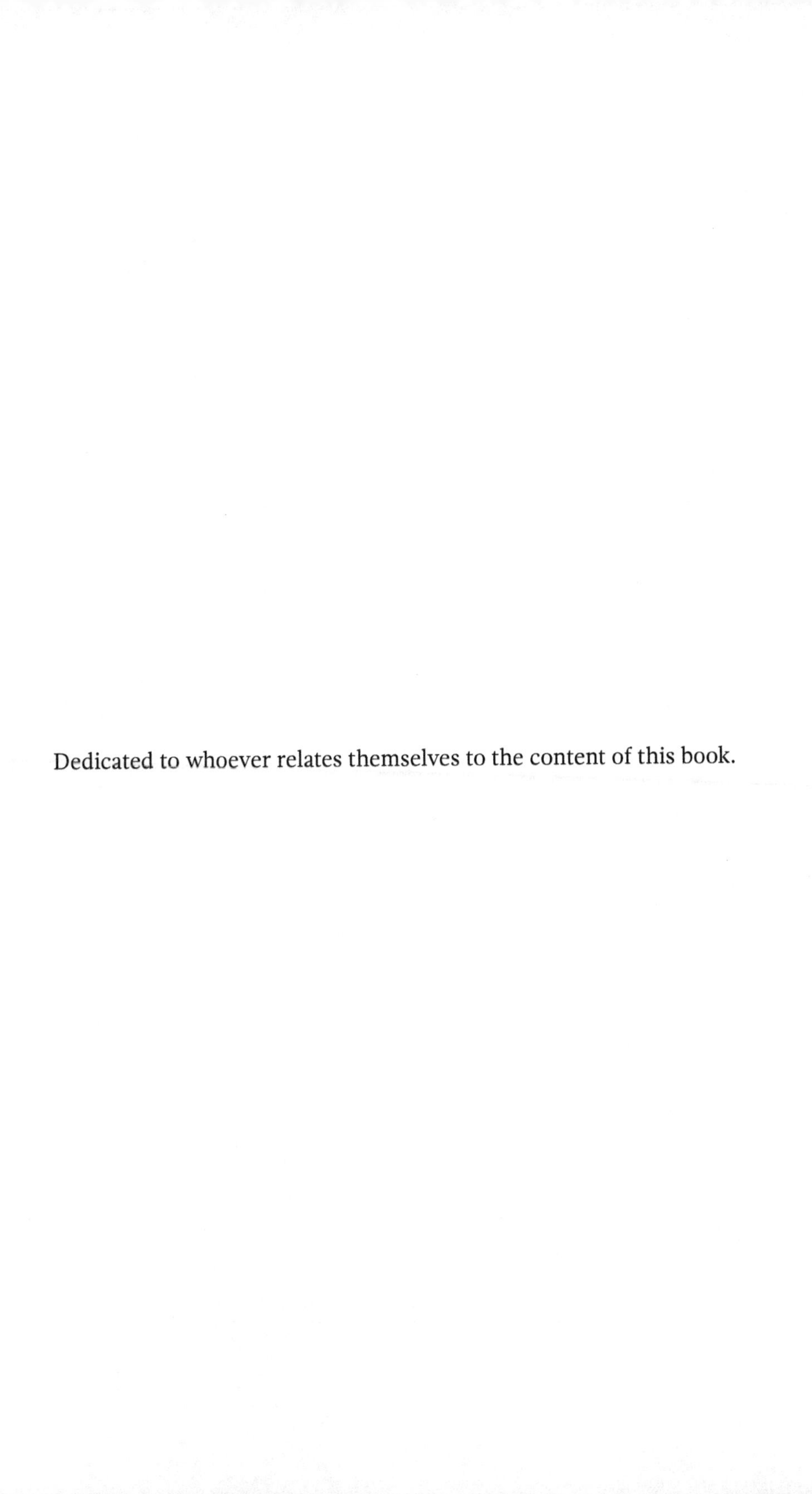

Dedicated to whoever relates themselves to the content of this book.

Contents

Preface   *vii*

Prologue   *ix*

1. The Loss   1

2. Journey Of Terror   5

3. Fighting Alone   8

4. Clash With Yourself   12

5. Puppet Of Their Hands   16

6. Right Behind Your Back   20

7. The Reality And The Realization   23

The Messege   25

Preface

Author's Preface

This book is specially written for everybody despite their age, gender, colour, height, weight, mentality, education and culture. That is because this book is a self-realization, knowledge for all. The book consists of observational lessons that are for all and are great questions to ourselves. The book is purely a creation of writer and is result of knowledge gained by life experiences after the struggling years starts.

While we go forward in the journey of life we see and experience a lot of beautiful and scary things. But the more we take life seriously, the harder it gets. No doubt the experiences and knowledge we get throughout this journey should be taken seriously while the hurt, hate, happiness, harm, everything is temporary and are states of our own mind. Once we understand the reality of our life, we can see how wrong we have done to ourselves and others. This needs to be stopped and that's why a proper knowledge about our deeds should be provided.

The thoughts and views of the author might be different than what you might have learnt in your life but that is how it works, give it a try, look at your life through the lessons that author has provided here in this book. If you try to understand it on a deeper level you will be able to see a different face of your life and yourself. And because all of us have been so busy living our materialistic lives, we forgot to love ourselves and spread love around us. So, when we forget to live the way, we should, which we all are here for, we need to change our minds in order to see life in a totally blissful way.

Hoodwinker is not only a word, it is a position that we give to ourselves. Hoodwinker which means cheater or betrayer is the name we give to ourselves when we cheat ourselves knowingly or unknowingly. It is when we know we are in need and still we don't help ourselves or don't do things to make our lives better. We are the reason to create trouble in our own lives.

All of us are so deeply involved in our materialistic lives that we don't take our well being seriously, some of us might be having mental problems, physical problems, and might not know that we also have a spiritual life to take care of. But that is not the point here, the point is that we need to forget how-to-live in order to learn how to actually live. Sometimes we need to forget things that doesn't serve us anymore. And because the world is so large, life is too short to get stuck on a single problem. And that is why this book is here, to help you understand yourself in a different dimension. The way we are stuck in life, we are totally unaware of the power inside us which can make us free from all the fuss in our lives and set our wings in the higher level of the sky.

There is still a lot to be seen, to be experienced and to be lived, so don't waste life just like that and change yourself in a positive way. Don't be afraid but surrender to life and it will take you to the beautiful destinations never explored. That is what life is all about exploring, so keep exploring it.

Author's word: I dedicate this book to each and every person in this world who is busy thinking that God has made their life tough and so it be, which is not true. While reading this book, I request you to forget about everything and everyone for once and just focus on yourself no matter what, and once you complete this book then you choose to either make yourself better first and then others or you choose to get back to your normal life, it's all your choice. So, I request everyone to read this book and get the ultimate secret of self-improvement!

Prologue

How does a person cheat other?

Just by changing sides, not supporting when in need, being with someone else after promising to be together forever, by lying, refusing to give back what they took, giving a word and then turning back, breaking promises, back stabbing, and what not. If these are the ways people cheat others and you felt relatable reading it, then you might feel worse if you get to know how you cheat yourself, the person you love more than anything in this world. You might say you love someone else (your loved ones) more than yourself but that is where you start cheating yourself.

There is no chance that you can love another person more than yourself, that is because you are you, but you cannot love others and make themselves you. Complicated? Let me simplify it a bit. You were born alone, so there is no way that you can totally be another person. You can get attached to others, love others, help others, save others, educate others, you can be born from them or be born with them or be born for them but still remain an individual. You can not enlighten others but help them enlighten themselves by the knowledge you can provide, you can only enlighten yourself by taking knowledge. You can feed others but not fill their stomach by eating food by yourself, you can educate others but enlighten yourself only, you can do work for others but experience life by yourself only. The idea of being an individual is that your life is in your hand, your experience is only yours.

It is beyond horrible when you cheat yourself, but that doesn't mean cheating others isn't horrible, it is. But the biggest sin one can do is to betray themselves. Here, what I mean by betraying is different than what one does to others around them. And that's why this book is all about realizing the amount of wrong we do to us and others around us and how not to do it. It doesn't mean everybody who will read this book will change themselves quickly just by reading the book, but some lessons and some changes could help change many minds. And there are some changes that you and only you can apply in your life in order to change your life and be true to yourself and people around you.

Life is far greater than just being in a well filled with little bit of ground water in which you're swimming like a little fish. Life is the ocean yet to be explored by you. You can't go to every corner but swim freely, of course there will be troubles and threats but enjoying it all is what life is.

Let us move forward and understand how not to cheat ourselves by knowing what we are already doing which needs to be cancelled right there.

CHAPTER ONE

THE LOSS

We all lose things in our lives without realising that we own nothing in this world except ourselves. We all have experienced loss in our life. But then to not experience it again, we take precautions. And just like that, we lose ourselves too while pleasing the world, but then why don't we take precautions to avoid losing ourselves?

If you observe, a person is always afraid to lose everything except the precious one of them all, their own self! They would take precautions and actions to save everything else but not themselves. It is not others cheating us, we are the hoodwinkers of our own lives.

Is it easy to recover the loss of loved ones? If not, then why would you put yourself in a place that you lose yourself? Self-care/self-love doesn't only mean taking care of your body, keeping yourself happy and feeding yourself with pleasurable food. Self-love includes having such a strong bond with self that you don't feel alone when you are with yourself, you do not need anyone when you are with yourself, you take care of yourself and don't lose yourself because of anybody. Just like dead humans, dead personalities don't return and if you have a natural personality, it's your duty to preserve your innocence and your natural love for yourself.

Once you lose yourself, nobody is responsible for your loss but you. We blame people who act tough and mean but keeping ourself stable is totally in our hand. Why would you want to give your remote control to someone else if you don't like to watch the channel they enjoy? And I am not telling you to blame yourself, but take credit of your own mistakes instead of blaming others.

Enough of this stuff, but a rational person would go through worse and still come out better because they know how not to lose their self in times of struggle but learn from it. They would absorb every single drop of knowledge out of every situation and then shape themselves accordingly.

Keeping it simple as that LESSON NO. 1-

"In hard times, either come out stronger and wiser or fight till you become better but don't lose yourself before and after you pass the test!"

Either you learn or you stay there until you learn your lesson is a better way to shape and save yourself from a big loss. Because being good, vulnerable and weak at times is okay, but that should not stop you from growing stronger and should not force you to lose yourself and that is why sometimes walking away, staying silent and ignoring is the best way to let go of some not so worthy matters, situations and people.

Know what is precious and what is not and then prioritize it accordingly even if some of your not so precious things get upset. Your duty is to handle your emotions, thoughts, actions and life not to handle others'. When you start to focus on what is essentially more important for you, your life will drastically change in a positive way. You do not have to focus on others, it is not your duty to keep everyone happy all the time. Do not be a people pleaser, be practical.

"The loss is not always about losing something, it is also about giving the wrong things to wrong people at the wrong time."

There are many types of loss if we jump into it, but that's not the matter here.

It is like, people keep losing something every day in their life. But there are only few things that they truly care about. Few of them are, money, loved ones, precious expensive things and life. While these are the few main things a person would care about in their life, there are many things forbidden. A person would care more for money rather than career, because career is a pathway towards money while money is a destination for them. When we tap into these things, we get to know that people have already lost their rational thinking and morals of life.

One might or might not believe this, but losing a person is not as horrible as losing yourself. From beginning to round it always comes to losing yourself. When I talk about losing yourself, it doesn't only mean losing your personality. Losing yourself is an experience one could never forget.

First of all, accept yourself howouver you are, and if there are some corrections to do, do it. Improve yourself but never hate yourself if you know you are a good person.

I have seen people lose themselves in reality much horribly than anyone could even imagine. But that doesn't mean to get insecure in being there for people, being attached to someone, or sacrificing for people. You can do all of it for the worthy ones indeed but everytime you have to be careful and smart enough to understand people's intentions. The money, the love, the people you lost are maybe or maybe not coming back, but you have only you everytime. See yourself higher than your ego or pride. You are something more than you have ever realised and that is what makes you different than everyone else. When you know your ego and expand it, you become more powerful than you know. Your ego is not I, your ego is I am for everyone, I see myself in everyone and everyone is my own. That is when you stop getting bothered by people and instead of losing yourself.

The thing is, people are ready to lose themselves and that is what costs them more than anything. Although some things are meant to be lost and it is necessary to let go of some people and things away in order to make your own life better. Loss only occurs when you are more attached to something or someone than you should. Until you are not so much emotionally attached with something or someone, you won't be affected if they're gone or if it's lost. We make ourselves so much vulnerable that we forget to keep things in limits and once the limits are crossed, then the side effects start taking place and then nobody is to be blamed except you.

Although, you should sacrifice for love, family and friends if and only if they are worthy of it. Know who is worthy of what and then do what is for them. You would not know how to do it until and unless you start taking pauses and time to think about things rationally. When you take time to make decisions, you give yourself time to think the right way, calm any unwanted feelings down, stop your emotions right there and start thinking from your mind. And the more you do this, your body is being used to not use emotions while taking important decisions or when they are not worthy. Your emotions are a channel to express yourself, but they cannot help you take decisions, they are only and only inner emotional garbage getting out through various ways and it has nothing to do with decision making.

The only moral of this chapter is to learn not to lose yourself, learn to let go of everything that bothers you more than you can tolerate when it is not worthy, and to change the mentality that you can have attachments out of your limits. Sometimes we are responsible for our own pain and hurt, it's our decisions that are putting us in such situations and therefore being in your senses is much needed. At last, you now have understood that your life and loss is all in your hand, and nobody else deserves the remote control.

You have your life because you are the only worthy ruler of your life and nobody else.

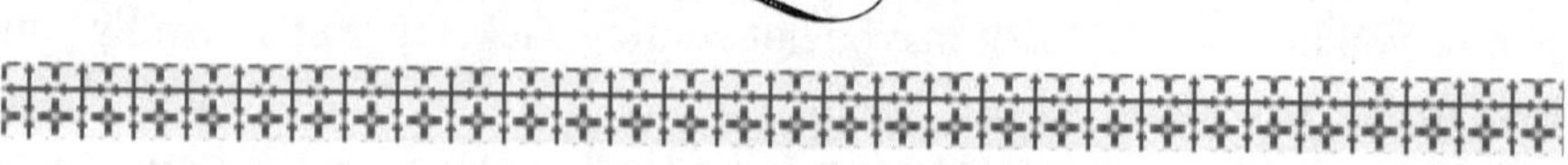

CHAPTER TWO

JOURNEY OF TERROR

Fear and terror are cousins from the same family. Fear might be gone at a time, but terror leaves a trauma behind. I heard someone say, Life is a journey full of terror. Little did I knew; life is all in your hands so don't let others decide what will scare you and what not. You might have seen people believing what others say to them, instead of doing their own research they tend to believe everything they listen to, see or feel. You have to do your own research before even believing others blindly because everybody has a different point of viewing things and different perspectives and meanings of things, situations and life.

For people, terror is when change occurs. If you take change as something bad, it will turn out to be bad but if you take change in a positive way, it is all you need to step ahead in your life. Sometimes the terror is all about not knowing your own power. You don't need to be saved or to be rescued by anybody, you just need the knowledge of your own power and how to access it. You might think you are unable to tap into your potential to the fullest but the thing is that you don't give your hundred percent believing in yourself that you can achieve anything once you keep your mind into it.

Your life is not a journey of terror at the first place, it's a platform to learn and experience everything and know yourself better in situations that you haven't expected. Your life is your biggest teacher that teaches you the things nobody else can. In the previous chapter, I have explained about loss, the loss that should be focused on. In this chapter I am willing to take your focus to the word 'fear'. What fear actually is? We all have different definitions of fear. Some might say it is phobia, dislike, or a feeling, anything it can be. But the thing is, fear is just an illogical state of mind which is result of stress, tension and anxiety. Fear is when we take some things more seriously than we should. Again, people's perspective can be different than what I have written, but it is just to give a different perspective to people.

While we are alert and, in our senses, it is impossible for fear to take place in our mind. The main point here is that most of the time we are so into everything else that we forget to understand what is going on inside us. You can surely overcome your fear because this little feeling in your mind can affect you till an extent only, after that its effects are no more bothering you. The thing is that fear is temporary uneasiness which goes away by itself once our perspective changes about the matter. That is the only difference between fear and terror, terror can be permanent and leave a trauma in your head so easily.

Again, when trauma is there in your mind, you are unaware of your own self in such a way that you keep exhausting the energy of your mind and body by focusing on the worst things. I will say fear is nothing but lack of alertness and misunderstandings with your own self, but terror and trauma are real. Nearly 9 out of 10 people are suffering through different types of traumas in their lives silently fighting it with a bright smile on their face. I will call it cheating to self, it is because if you need to hide it, it is worse than you think of it and that's when you need help to solve it and overcome it. No matter how hard you try, trauma cannot be easily sorted out by yourself, you need love, care and positivity around you to get familiar with your trauma but then how will you sort it out?

LESSON NO. 2 -

"You cannot solve your trauma or run from it, but you can be familiar with your trauma, understand it's cause and release it all and make a nice agreement with your trauma of not being bothered by it anymore and by going easy on yourself and your trauma both."

You don't need to hate your trauma and be afraid of it. If it is caused by terror then fear will only add fuel to it. So, doing a nice agreement of not being bothered anymore. caring about it, going easy on with your trauma will be a good start for you to simply let it go. You cannot let go of it all at once so you have to make peace with your trauma and make it your friend, not your enemy.

Talking about peace reminded me of how we need to make peace with uneasiness, hate, hurt, and everything or everyone that's bothering us. While you make peace with everything that is being a problem in your life, you are releasing half of your trauma out of your mind leading to a peaceful life. There is nothing more expensive than peace these days. Taking care of your peace is much more important than anything else. Once you are at peace, you can put your focus in yourself for your own betterment.

Fear can mostly be your weakness and in rare case it will be your strength. It is better to not let your fear rule over your emotions and make you backoff. Your fear and trauma will make you isolated, and that is not life if it limits your growth and progress. Everything which is there to stop your growth is either teaching you to hustle harder or is there to get destroyed by you. And there should be no fear if you start understanding things, people and situation more because you know why it is happening and the solution is on your fingertips then.

People being stressed is just a start, they would not take control of their emotions but let their emotions control them. It is taught to all of us that we should aways be nice, but nobody taught us that we should speak up if the niceness is the reason we are suffering. Why will anybody take control of your life if you do not let them to? Thinking straight into this, let go, speak up or fight if it makes you suffer but do not be afraid of anything but yourself. Your bond with yourself should be strong enough that you can control yourself when needed and not give anybody else a chance to tolerate your toxicity. Do not let yourself be toxic but do not even tolerate others' toxicity.

Again, you are to make yourself better first then only you can help your loved ones or others. Without focusing on yourself, you cannot focus on others. They say, first find yourself and then help others. A flawed person cannot help others be perfect. And once you understand this, you will start to focus on what needs your attention first and it will lead you to wisdom.

At the end of the day, there is no fear and no terror if you know your power and how to use it correctly and properly. Who fears others when the monster is inside them? Control your inner monster, use its power for something great. Be prideful of course but do not let it turn into ego. Your pride is you and not the things you do!

CHAPTER THREE

Fighting Alone

Why in the first place are you even fighting? Who you are fighting with? And what are you fighting for?

Question these to yourself and seek answers by yourself. The more you ask questions the more you learn and the clearer it gets for you. When we say fighting alone, it is just like trying to survive but not live the life. Being grateful to what you have ignoring what you need or don't have which you are struggling to get is all so cliche. The thing is, why do you need to ignore the bad part? By focusing on yourself I don't mean only focusing on the good part. When you focus on everything, you learn to let go of what you don't need, create space for what you need and then get what you need. Again, wanting and needing are two different things. You want something because you like it, you need something because it is essential & important for you. Focus on needs your first. When you learn to focus on everything equally, you are not fighting anymore in your life.

Focusing on everything at first will only make you understand what is not worth your focus and what needs your focus. It is like giving a f#ck about everything is not good for you. And it is okay if people are upset because you don't give a f#ck about each and every kind of bullpotty they do. Okay, jokes apart, you should know everything but not care about everything and waste your energy fighting to every baseless illogical thing. It is not so amazing to have mental health issues, if you have them sort them out because they are not so cool to brag about your mental health issues. It will eventually just make you miserable as the time passes by.

I have seen people struggling, I myself have struggled, but who doesn't? There is no need to be embarrassed if you are struggling for anything. Take things easy and stop struggling, get your moves smarted and thug it out instead of going through stress and being hard on yourself. You cannot skip hard work in everything but you should where you can. Hard work is only to increase your physical with mental potential whereas smart work is to increase your mental potential. Now as yourself one more question, what in the world is wrong with you that you are stressing so much about everything? Once you find the answer, you need to stop stressing yourself and taking tension by burdening yourself.

While you are learning, struggle is there to improve you. But if you are still struggling after struggling for so long, you need to stop struggling. It might sound pretty complicated but once you're learning period is completed you can still continue learning but stop struggling. It is like you have completed your struggles and schooling at 20 but you are still struggling in your 30s because now you got a habit of putting yourself in trouble and choosing the struggling way always. Know that nobody is your enemy, nobody is your competition and it is all you focusing on you.

You really need to look back once and see where you have come from and how far you have reached. See the struggles you have faced, the fears you have overcome and then how powerful you have become. You also have to implement all you have learnt, not only take the knowledge but turn it into wisdom by actually understanding it. It is like turbulence should shake you but not your wisdom which is your great power.

Unlearning what you have learnt is not the thing you should do. Do not believe everything you learn until you apply it in your life. And do not create a solid perspective on anything because you need to know everything in order to decide what is right for you. You think you are alone when nobody is with you, hear me out, your learnings and knowledge is always going to help you more than any human could. They don't say it casually that books are your best friends, they actually become when you understand everything written in them for your own self-improvement.

When you are open to every kind of knowledge and information, you shape your mind in such a way that you no more take useless matters seriously. With this being open and understanding to everything also changes your point of view, perspective and your personality because you have already learnt what to do, how to do and when to do. See, it is a nice thing to keep improving yourself, but whatever you do should be for you and should not harm others, good if it benefits others and you at the same time.

If you find a wise person someday, do not take anything from them except their knowledge and wisdom. It will add some more content into your mind. For most of your problems, books are available as solutions. When you think you are fighting alone, remember everybody is fighting alone only. One can help you in your fight but cannot fight your war with you. Taking help is not a shameful thing, expecting someone to fight your war is. And if you stop thinking of it as a war it will be better for you.

To be really rude but honest, you are a fool to think that life is a war and you are a fighter, LOL. You are nothing, your problems are nothing in front of the actual and real ones. But again, do not supress your emotions, let them come out at once, then start taking everything as a lesson and start learning. Forget what you were taught, Einstein's formulas, Newton's theories, periodic table, to tally the balance sheet, what so ever, just forget it all. Learn what life is trying to teach you. Instead of learning how earth, stuff in and on earth, and stuff around the earth works, first of all, learn how you and your life works, learn your own mechanism first, not only biology I mean but also the stuff about how practicality would help you. Have some knowledge about yourself first, nobody cares about how the earth works, its earth's problem to understand its work until and unless you are really eager to hop into earth's business. Hold on to your business first, let the other things do their work.

To keep it very simple and normal, you have to understand a few things very deeply which are to make you worry less and live more. When you grow up, start taking money matters in your hands and when you start worrying about what will happen in future, you start to cheat yourself just that moment. When you stop believing in yourself and your potential, you already fall down levels below. Being self-critic is the main problem of people these days. Ask yourself one more question, would anybody believe in you if you are not sure about yourself? They won't, right? And then you go seek other's respect and support without getting your own support? It is like asking others to help you stand up and then you yourself not willing to stand up.

LESSON NO. 3 -

"Do not expect help, trust and support from others if you do not provide it to yourself."

When you are not with yourelf why do you think others will be with yourself? Make an agreement with yourself, do not break your bond with yourself. Do not beg, be powerful enough that you ask and it is done and why beg when you realise that you have ultimate power inside? Keep asking yourself questions, and search for your answers. Do not let the outside influences make you break your bond with yourself.

With this lesson you will understand yourself better and even if anybody else is not supporting you, there is no reason to hate them because it is totally your duty to be your supporter, everybody else are not responsible or bound to be your supporter. Fighting alone is not at all meaningful when you are living a peaceful life.

CHAPTER FOUR

CLASH WITH YOURSELF

If only you are a self-critic. No! no matter if you are a self-critic or not, once or more than once you definitely had a clash with yourself. Everybody does and it is not a rare thing. Most of the time people (mostly adult and teenagers) keep having an inner fight with themselves. It is as normal as having a fight with your sibling or friend. But when you do it too much, something in you changes. Fighting with yourself is not bad, sometimes you need to do it, what is bad is that you criticize yourself to such an extent that you lose all the hope. When you fight with yourself it is a good indication of you having a healthy relationship with yourself as you are communicating with yourself.

The thing is that I am keeping this book simple as hell and with only a few pages of content and no short stories is because I want to keep it all straight and simple for each of you to understand. No complicated shit, no long talks, just to the point stuff. More to the point stuff, more understanding, more learning.

When do you clash with your own self and how? It can be in anyway, the ways we do not even realize. At once you would try to teach and explain yourself why not to do certain things and the other second you would scold yourself because you still did it. Believe it or not but we do treat ourselves like an innocent kid who doesn't understand anything. It is adorable how we take care of ourselves and it is totally okay to scold, taunt or fight yourself at times as it also gives you decision taking power.

Situations play a big role over here. Sometimes you are not supposed to behave like you are told to do and sometimes you are supposed to behave just like you have been told. You clearly are a learner but not a servant. You are supposed to do what you should do at the moment, not what someone tells you to do. Yes, if somebody tell you to do what you should, indeed do it but you should know what to do and when to do. It doesn't come to your mind just like that, you need to shape yourself with experience enough that you can fluently take right decisions. Even if the decisions are wrong, they teach you something valuable.

Why do you need to give a reaction on everything when you can just ignore and mind your own business on a go? Key to happiness is only when you mind your business more and don't indulge in useless matters. Also, a reason to keep this book free from hard words and complicated sentences so that you can clearly understand that I am teaching you clear straight things to mind your business for your own happiness. Would you, do it? Of course, if you want to be happy you have to do it.

See, when you start taking knowledge from everything, you will have enough experiences to gain enough wisdom by yourself. You don't need to pay fees and go learn life lessons, your life and nature are giving you free experiences and lessons, take the advantage and learn as much as you can.

The thing that I call clashing with yourself is not only about fighting with yourself on some topic. This is such a big subject to explain. If I go on explaining, there is a lot. But here I am explaining a few lessons which are essential. Fighting with yourself is -

1. Struggling to improve things in you
2. Trying to keep yourself out of mess
3. Trying to keep yourself in control
4. Encouraging yourself
5. Stopping yourself/Limiting yourself

there are many more which are not essential for this chapter but are surely mentioned in the next few chapters.

Recently, it is all about immature people calling themselves mature and then not knowing anything about their own self. Funny, how people think they know it all but doesn't even know themselves properly yet. I mean just think once, what have you even done yet if you do not even know yourself well? What are you, a brainless animal who just eats, sleeps, excretes and repeats? If you call yourself civilized enough, live like a human first. And if you don't want to, stop calling yourself civilised, you're just an animal in a concrete jungle. You are not to be blamed, it is what you have been taught since your childhood and you can do nothing about it but forget it and start learning what you need in your life.

You might have understood by the sentences only that you fight with yourself and these 5 are the main reasons. You would mostly engage in a fight with yourself because of these reasons. It is all your v/s you. Nobody is your biggest enemy except you and nobody is your bests friend except you. It is just like ITADORI YUJI having SUKUNA RYOMEN inside at a minute and then it is like PRAHLAD having NARSIMHA inside the other minute. I would not go into historical literatures and anime deeply but if you know about both the stories, you would understand it better. But you might have heard or read this quote - You spend most of your life inside your head, make sure it is a nice place to be. It is just like that, make sure your inner goodness is more than your outer beauty. But also, be wise enough to show your good side and bad side where you should.

Each and every person is made up with accuracy, if you believe in God or not but whoever has created everything has created everything accurately and precisely at their places. It is like evil are right on their side and the good are right on their side, the creator has left no mistake in anything, everything is right at its place. Do what you think is right but be ready to face the side effects and fruits of your karma. You have to be confident about what you do, know yourself better that your intentions are good enough and trust yourself that you will do what is good for you and doesn't harm others around you. And once you know yourself, why would you be afraid of karma? You know you will reap what you sow, why worry about something you already know?

The evils do their work, the goodies do their work, both create the balance in the world. This balance is needed in everything. While love can make even the evilest of the evils turn good, just like that, the hate & jealousy can make even the nicest people go evil. It is all balanced together. If you would not struggle, you will not gain wisdom, turn out to be a fool, and a fool cannot live without other's help. The struggles you face, they are not only your teacher but artists to shape you into a beautifully perfect (at your level) art. Let the artists do their work, give yourself a chance, let yourself turn into a majestic butterfly.

LESSON NO. 4 -

"You do not need to be like others and create an imbalance in your life, whatever you are at right now is where you should be, do what you should and eventually you will reach where you are meant to be, where you deserve to be."

Your karma plays a big role in it, what you deserve depends on your karma, your life is all in your life. Believe it or not but you create and control your own karma and you create your own problems, even if you haven't you can cut the problems off and/or ignore them, or take actions to sort them out but not rant about it.

The work of creator was to create, now your life is totally yours, you decide what to do and nobody else would take the charge of your life. Do not fight, live!

CHAPTER FIVE

PUPPET OF THEIR HANDS

Famous late star Rajesh Khanna sir had said these lines "**ZINDAGI EK RANGMANCH HAI AUR HAM SAB IS RANG MANCH PAR KATHPUTLIYAN HAI, HAM SABKI DORR UPAR WALE KE HAATH MEIN HAI, KAB KISKI DOR KHICH JAYE KOI NAHI JANTA**" and in other dialogue he has said, "**MAUT TOH EK PAL HAI**". I do respect the words he has said, they indeed make sense. But make sure not to go deep in it. These are just some philosophical movie dialogues which are far more different than reality of your life. Everybody has a different life, not even a single life would be similar to other, we all have our unique time. And these dialogues cannot be applied to each and every life on earth.

Similarly, all of us have given our lives to something or someone and have become puppets. People do not like it when they are ordered to do something, they do not want to become servants but they are indirectly or directly doing everything and have become puppets already. Believe it or not, you do what others want, not what you want. Is it how you really want your life to work? If not, then you need to wake up from your sweet dreams sleep and start getting more practical. Many of you might have made rules for your own selves in your life to stay a better person, but sometimes those rules limit you and you need to break them in order to progress forward.

It is obvious to remain in your boundaries, but sometimes you have to break them. Rajput in 7th century till now have remained under their rules but were killed by Mughals and other Muslim emperors and opponents by deceiving them which cost them their lives, but if the rules were broken and a level-to-level fight would have been given to the Mughals then the story would've turned different. Meanwhile on the other side, Maurya emperors did what Chanakya told and taught them and conquered whole India at a time. The difference was that Chanakya neeti was all about making and breaking rules when needed for the good, and that everything is acceptable in war and politics which helped the Mauryans more than expected.

I would like to go Chanakya way, rules are indeed needed to control yourself from doing the wrong but sometimes to do right you need to break them for the betterment of everyone around you including you. Being as practical as Chanakya would not only help you think rationally and logically but would change your life drastically in a beneficial way. More emotions in life only causes pain while adding logic to life keeps your emotions at a pause and saves you from having pain and emotional trauma. You can find the book of Chanakya Neeti in book stores nearby in order to understand the practicality and apply it on your life.

If you do not know how you are being a puppet, you should start saying no. I would recommend a book for this too - The art of saying No by Damon Zahariades and How to Tell No Without Saying No by R. Kesavamurthy. There are many books regarding this topic which you can search about and read. Saying no is not rude always, it is a word to make people set boundaries between you and them. Saying no is also the first step of self-care. When you say no fluently, you are not allowing others to make you do what they want which will bother you later. Saying no means refusing to become a puppet, it is okay to help people only when it is very much necessary, only if that person deserves it, only if they are truly asking and needing help. All the other times you are saying no to stop anybody from controlling you and bothering you. And it is not bad to say no, it is healthy if it is fluent.

It is not obvious to only be puppets of people directly, sometimes you are puppets to them as their customers, audience, users, consumers, anything. The products and things they create for you will influence you in some way that either you will like it, love it or get obsessed to it or you would start doing what you see, or maybe you would start doing what the influencers tell you, ask you or advertise you to do isn't it? What is it? Any kind of obsession or addiction or attachment to outside things would just make you a puppet to them. 'Them' can be anyone, the business professionals & the companies/organizations, the actors & influencers, the advertisers, the politicians, the doctors, the producers of products, movies or anything that you watch, consume or buy. These are the highers who are willing to control you in the name of support and you are falling into their traps proudly.

And why would you want to fall in such traps and be puppets to their hands? Even the creator, call it God, nature, anything, it also does not control you and your life, the highest authority (the creator) has given your life in your hands so that you can control it, shape it and do what is right according to you and for you. But we are so brainwashed that we do not see what is essential and what is a trap, we just keep going on according to the ones who are trapping us for their personal benefits. You know it, still you do not do anything to stop giving your control in their hands. This is when you become the hoodwinker to yourself. Those who trap you are surely hoodwinkers, but why do you have to involve with them and become another deceiver to yourself?

Even those people discussing all way about self-love does not know even one percent of what love for self is while they keep fooling themselves saying such sweet sugar-coated things and deceive their subconscious self-ruining their whole life. **Your obsessions and FOMO has already made you become puppets, your fear of missing out (FOMO) and other addictions and obsessions of following and being up to date with trends has made you so blind that you have forgot what living life actually is.** Since, either you have become blind or are sleeping and living in sweety dreamy life, you are missing out on your own life. The time passes by but there is nothing that you can do to stop it, it doesn't stop for anybody, and nobody can stop it, neither time nor your karma.

LESSON NO. 5 -

"Stop being puppets, wake up, see your life in a different way and take control of your own life instead of giving it to your comfort zones, addictions/obsessions/attachments and FOMO. You are the ruler of your life and rulers fight for their thrones not give it to anybody."

Tell me one thing, if you were a King/Queen who has the throne all by themselves, what would you do? Rule it or give it to someone else? Of course, rule it right? You are already a King/Queen or we can say ruler of your own life, the control is all in your hands, you choose what to do and what not to, why would you give the control to others just like that? And blaming God or the creator is not valid, you are the ruler not them, blame yourself and improve your life instead of falling in such cheap traps created by money minded monsters.

You have the potential which you are not aware of, you need to take a pause, look inside you, analyse yourself, correct yourself, improve yourself and then continue with life. It is okay to take breaks if needed, but working your ass off under a company or organization run by some riches and then living a middle class or upper middle-class life is just higher level of professional slavery that you are doing. Do what you want, what you need, what you dream is, you have slept a lot then must have dreamt of something right? Do keep a goal in your life which improves you and your life. Not having a solid goal in life in other words is just being a slave and puppet to others. And I know, nobody would like to be a puppet or a slave if they realise what they are going through. So, turn your dreams into goals and then aim it and achieve it.

Everyone deserves a chance to get out of this puppet life and be free of it. Everybody needs materialistic freedom until they realise it is all a trap and the real freedom is something different. Don't be a hoodwinker to yourself, be true, honest and a well-wisher to yourself. And mainly do not be hoodwinked by the monsters out there. You deserve what you set your mind to, if you would not deserve it, you would never dream about it, you think of it because your subconscious mind knows that you deserve what you dreamt of until and unless it doesn't harm you and others.

You know you deserve it, that is why you want it. Hustle hard and improve yourself until you achieve it!

CHAPTER SIX

RIGHT BEHIND YOUR BACK

People will definitely be sweet on your face. And then would badmouth about you on your back. Sweet on outside, devil's advocate inside! Nobody would like to live with such people if they knew how they do backbitch others. It is overwhelmingly irritating, but what to do, we cannot change people. I had learnt it somewhere, when someone is behaving bad to you - if they are your loved ones, accept them, understand them, provide them love, talk to them and sort it out. If they are common people, you regularly see or meet, accept them, talk it out and try understanding their problem if it doesn't work then slow down the communication. If they are stranger, ignore and move. But in every case, accept that person, accept their behaviour and then act accordingly.

If they are bothering you, speak it out, talk it out and if it still does not stop, take the right action accordingly. Not always that you have to fight and argue with people, sometimes ignorance and distance is more beneficial to you. It is not about what they do, it is about what affects you. Let people do their karma, take care of your own peace. The more peace you get, the closer you get to yourself, the more powerful you become from inside. Your mind captures knowledge more when it is at peace. See, to be honest, your life is all about learning, and that is what matters the most, what you learn. Your learnings decide your personality, behaviour, and energy surrounding you.

First things first, you do not owe anyone any kind of explanation or answer until and unless it is necessary for you to reply. Being clear, people will go down to such an extent to make you argue with them and to frustrate the shit out of you, this is how they want to control you. First, they mess up with your mind and then, they make you say things out of frustration which will make you look bad. But as I mentioned in previous chapter, you have full control over yourself and your life, you decide what to respond and how to respond. You are the creator of your karma, why would you lower your standards to such a level where you have to be mean and crazy over someone else's words?

I remember, my mother used to tell me, **do not argue, speak with your actions!** And I started doing it when I started living in another city alone, I knew, I do not need to give answers to everyone cause my silence would be a nice answer. But I do not need to stay silent on everything. I did stay away from arguments as much as I could, but when you need to speak up and take a stand for yourself or the innocents, you should not back off. The worst thing you could do is sit back and let people bother you with their ugly plans. Here, using your wisdom and smartness is very much needed. No matter how good the other person tries to be, if they are wrong and bothering you, fluently take a stand for yourself. No need to shout, just some fluent mind opening words and the other person would know that you do understand what wrong they are doing to you.

LESSON NO. 6 -

"Stay away from arguments as long as they are not essential enough, but do not back off when you should take a stand for the right thing to stop people from bothering you because you do not owe answers to everyone but surely should speak up when needed."

This lesson is two targets one bullet thing which is two in one lesson. Arguments just ruin your mind and frustrate you. People might think you backed off if you did not reply in an argument, but that is okay let people think whatever they want, your peace of mind is more important than proving your point in a useless argument. I mean, it is entertainment for them, ruin it, ruin their entertainment because who cares if they get their entertainment or not, there are plenty of drama movies to watch, do not create one and become part of one to give people their desired entertainment for free.

When you do not argue back, you do disappoint people and save yourself a plenty of time and energy to focus on important things. Being emotional is not the best thing you should do in front of people. Your emotions are a substitute of fun for others, and when you do not let them have fun with your emotions, they would surely get disappointed and bad mouth you behind your back but why do you care? let them do their low-level shit and keep focusing on improving your personality, knowledge and standards high.

It is okay to be emotional, but a simple thing I would tell you is not to show your weakness to anyone except your parents. Everyone else would surely want to use your weakness against you. Believe it or not, nobody is actually your friend, they play friends until and unless you step in their territory and violate their boundaries, then you are screwed. If you do not trust me, try it and experience it by yourself. I would not ask you to believe even a single word written in this book, try it yourself if you do not believe it.

This chapter is personally based on my own experience and plenty other real examples which I have seen people experience. Meanwhile, you can sit back and enjoy people getting disappointed when you refuse to argue back and make a fool out of them. Because most of the people doesn't know that disappointing people by not providing them with their kind of entertainment is more important than responding back to a fool in an argument. Let the fools sink in the puddle while you focus on the path ahead!

CHAPTER SEVEN

THE REALITY AND THE REALIZATION

It gets too late before you realise what you have done or what has happened to you. Sometimes reality and realisation are interconnected. You might have thought your life out and the mistakes you are making or have made in your life. You are not at all bound to understand of apply whatever I have written over here. But you can think it all out and then decide what is best for you and that is what the motive of this book is. To let yourself have the charge of your life is to be responsible for whatever happens in your life. It is better to realise it before it is too late!

When a human is born, they rely on its parents until it grows up into adult, then the adult relies on money, people, everything else until it's too late to realise that all these times it had the power to take charge of its life. And those people who try to take charge of their own lives are known as rebels, but it is much better to be called a rebel than to be dependent on others. The earlier you realise things, the better justice you do to yourself and your life. The reality you experience and the thing you think is reality are totally different than each other.

Sometimes, people are afraid to take the risk they need to make things better and it gets too late until they realise this. They realise, the life they missed, the life they didn't choose to live, the life they let go of and then it is too late to get back those opportunities. With jealousy in eyes, people see those who were struggling with them who got a good deal on life and are now living peacefully and then they regret not taking all the risk like the successful ones. It is that they don't understand that reality is different than their comfort zone. You have to leave your comfort zone and take risks, explore things in life and try giving yourself a chance to change your life and test your potential.

Until you do not give yourself a chance to prove yourself, you would never know how powerful you are. Not only physically but mentally and subconsciously too. The reality is something which if you understand then you can adore and if not then you will get wiped off by it. But fear would always block your blessings and would leave you lost in your comfort zone and never let you achieve what you deserve.

LESSON NO. 7 -

"Realise and unlock your potential before you realise that reality has hit you harder and before it is too late, take valuable risks to learn how to use your power and understand your potential."

You have power in you, all you need to do is to explore it out and learn how to use it in a beneficial way. The only thing you have to do is to think from your brain because your heart is for pumping blood and your gut is full of shit. You have a brain to use, the more you use it the more you learn, but make sure not to get confused as it would also confuse you between things but taking rational decision would help you out of confusion.

Decisions are totally work of your mind, do not let your emotional side ruin them. See, getting into trouble and having pain and hurt in life is only to keep balance in your life. Do not go all way over to seek happiness in everything else. Do what makes you happy and doesn't harm you and others. Most of the time people waste their time searching for joy later realising it was always in their hand to when to be happy and when to get hurt.

There is no meaning of late realization even if it is said that late realization is also accepted. The more you learn the more you realise what is needed at what time and hence it all makes things unfold and fall together in place. When you know your life is in your hand, why wait for God to make it all happen? The big guy is already busy in creating things or maybe asleep we never know. So, relying on someone we don't know is foolishness. Not to be a clown but take the charge and complete your duties.

And with this you have achieved the knowledge of 7 lessons from this book. I hope it helps you in a positive way!

The Messege

There is no meaning of reading this book if you cannot apply all these lessons in your own life. If in case you do not apply them, must give or sell this book to someone who would actually help themselves by applying these lessons in their life. I haven't written anything impossible to do things because these lessons are already applied in my life which helped me increase my wisdom level and understand my potential. First of all, it helped me find the lost me and then helped me improve my personality and then potential and then ultimate wisdom.

Somewhere I know there are no excuses to give because all these lessons are basic and can be easily applied to life if you are really willing to get out of your never-ending painful life and transform it into something more peaceful, joyful and meaningful. I have no reason spending months writing this book, planning its content all alone and completing it, it is all just to help others have what I found by myself. If I won't share my knowledge with people, it would go waste. But here, this book is all I am giving my audience as a gift to blissful life.

I cannot assure if it will influence everybody or not but I can surely assure that if people will apply these lessons in their lives, their lives would drastically change in a positive direction giving them the wisdom of experience and a different perspective to see life and this world. Again, know that you will see only what you will focus on so while taking important decisions of life, it is essential to not focus on any single thing but consider every way and analyse everything properly.

If this book actually helped you open the eyes of your brain, must join the campaign of hashtag **NOMOREAHOODWINKER** on social media platforms, especially our favourite one "Instagram" because it would give me a chance to see how this book have been helpful to my audience and to give us all a chance to connect with each other.

At last, it is us, us together in making the world a better place which can only happen once we are happy in our lives. And this is a sign to start hustling to make it all better and get out of your darkness into reality and give yourself a chance to live a better life ahead.

In this book, in any chapter, I have not influenced anyone to be rudely practical. Indeed, some people benefiting from your innocence would get hurt once you turn practical but being practical never includes being rude.

It is just being logical and rational without harming anyone and creating boundaries to not let people take advantage of your goodness. Help others but do not be fooled at any cost. Your grace should be in fluently creating boundaries and calmly stopping people from doing wrong to you and there is nothing bad in it. You seriously never have to be rude once you know how to calmly make people understand their mistake. Even in cases where they do not accept their mistake, distance is the answer. You are supposed to learn to protect your peace and be at peace being practically intelligent and having a constant control over your life.

This is the end! This is what you need to improve yourself from the scratch. Create your blessings yourself and then enjoy as you live free from stressful life and have a blissful life ahead!